FRANCIS FRITH'S

WIDNES
AND RUNCORN

PHOTOGRAPHIC MEMORIES

DOROTHY NICOLLE was born in Uganda and later lived in Hong Kong. She was educated in Belfast and at Leicester University where she attained a degree in British Archaeology and History. She has also lived in the Middle East and in France. This gypsy life has encouraged a love of Britain and its history so that, these days, she knows she has the perfect job – she is a Blue Badge Guide. She also lectures on various aspects of local and general history. Dorothy is married and now lives in Shropshire where she and her husband enjoy walking in the hills with their dogs.

FRANCIS FRITH'S
PHOTOGRAPHIC MEMORIES

WIDNES AND RUNCORN

PHOTOGRAPHIC MEMORIES

DOROTHY NICOLLE

First published in the United Kingdom in 2004 by
Frith Book Company Ltd

Limited Hardback Subscribers Edition Published in 2004
ISBN 1-85937-929-X

Paperback Edition 2004
ISBN 1-85937-854-4

British Library Cataloguing in Publication Data

Francis Frith's Widnes and Runcorn - Photographic Memories
Dorothy Nicolle

Frith Book Company Ltd
Frith's Barn, Teffont,
Salisbury, Wiltshire SP3 5QP
Tel: +44 (0) 1722 716 376
Email: info@francisfrith.co.uk
www.francisfrith.co.uk

Printed and bound in Great Britain

Front Cover: **WIDNES**, *St Paul's Church and Free Library
1908* 59503
Frontispiece: **WIDNES**, *West Bank 1923* 73918

*The colour-tinting is for illustrative purposes only, and is not intended
to be historically accurate*

CONTENTS

FRANCIS FRITH
VICTORIAN PIONEER

FRANCIS FRITH, founder of the world-famous photographic archive, was a complex and multi-talented man. A devout Quaker and a highly successful Victorian businessman, he was philosophical by nature and pioneering in outlook.

By 1855 he had already established a wholesale grocery business in Liverpool, and sold it for the astonishing sum of £200,000, which is the equivalent today of over £15,000,000. Now a very rich man, he was able to indulge his passion for travel. As a child he had pored over travel books written by early explorers, and his fancy and imagination had been stirred by family holidays to the sublime mountain regions of Wales and Scotland. 'What lands of spirit-stirring and enriching scenes and places!' he had written. He was to return to these scenes of grandeur in later years to 'recapture the thousands of vivid and tender memories', but with a different purpose. Now in his thirties, and captivated by the new science of photography, Frith set out on a series of pioneering journeys up the Nile and to the Near East that occupied him from 1856 until 1860.

INTRIGUE AND EXPLORATION

These far-flung journeys were packed with intrigue and adventure. In his life story, written when he was sixty-three, Frith tells of being held captive by bandits, and of fighting 'an awful midnight battle to the very point of surrender with a deadly pack of hungry, wild dogs'. Wearing flowing Arab costume, Frith arrived at Akaba by camel sixty years before Lawrence of Arabia, where he encountered 'desert princes and rival sheikhs, blazing with jewel-hilted swords'.

He was the first photographer to venture beyond the sixth cataract of the Nile. Africa was still the mysterious 'Dark Continent', and Stanley and Livingstone's historic meeting was a decade into the future. The conditions for picture taking confound belief. He laboured for hours in his wicker dark-room in the sweltering heat of the desert, while the volatile chemicals fizzed dangerously in their trays. Back in London he exhibited his photographs and was 'rapturously cheered' by members of the Royal Society. His reputation as a photographer was made overnight.

VENTURE OF A LIFE-TIME

Characteristically, Frith quickly spotted the opportunity to create a new business as a specialist publisher of photographs. He lived in an era of immense and sometimes violent change.

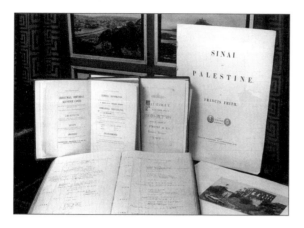

For the poor in the early part of Victoria's reign work was exhausting and the hours long, and people had precious little free time to enjoy themselves. Most had no transport other than a cart or gig at their disposal, and rarely travelled far beyond the boundaries of their own town or village. However, by the 1870s the railways had threaded their way across the country, and Bank Holidays and half-day Saturdays had been made obligatory by Act of Parliament. All of a sudden the working man and his family were able to enjoy days out and see a little more of the world.

With typical business acumen, Francis Frith foresaw that these new tourists would enjoy having souvenirs to commemorate their days out. In 1860 he married Mary Ann Rosling and set out on a new career: his aim was to photograph every city, town and village in Britain. For the next thirty years he travelled the country by train and by pony and trap, producing fine photographs of seaside resorts and beauty spots that were keenly bought by millions of Victorians. These prints were painstakingly pasted into family albums and pored over during the dark nights of winter, rekindling precious memories of summer excursions.

THE RISE OF FRITH & CO

Frith's studio was soon supplying retail shops all over the country. To meet the demand he gathered about him a small team of photographers, and published the work of independent artist-photographers of the calibre of Roger Fenton and Francis Bedford. In order to gain some understanding of the scale of Frith's business one only has to look at the catalogue issued by Frith & Co in 1886: it runs to some 670 pages, listing not only many thousands of views of the British Isles but also many photographs of most European countries, and China, Japan, the USA and Canada - note the sample page shown on page 9 from the hand-written Frith & Co ledgers recording the pictures. By 1890 Frith had created the greatest specialist photographic publishing company in the world, with over 2,000 sales outlets - more than the combined number that Boots and WH Smith have today! The picture on the next page shows the Frith & Co display board at Ingleton in the Yorkshire Dales (left of window). Beautifully constructed with a mahogany frame and gilt inserts, it could display up to a dozen local scenes.

POSTCARD BONANZA

The ever-popular holiday postcard we know today took many years to develop. In 1870 the Post Office issued the first plain cards, with a pre-printed stamp on one face. In 1894 they allowed other publishers' cards to be sent through the mail with an attached adhesive halfpenny stamp. Demand grew rapidly, and in 1895 a new size of postcard was permitted called the court card, but there was little room for illustration. In 1899, a year after Frith's death, a new card measuring 5.5 x 3.5 inches became the standard format, but it was not until 1902 that the divided back came into being, so that the address and message could be on one face and a full-size illustration on the other. Frith & Co were in the vanguard of postcard development: Frith's sons Eustace and Cyril continued their father's monumental task, expanding the number of views offered to the public and recording more and more places in Britain, as the

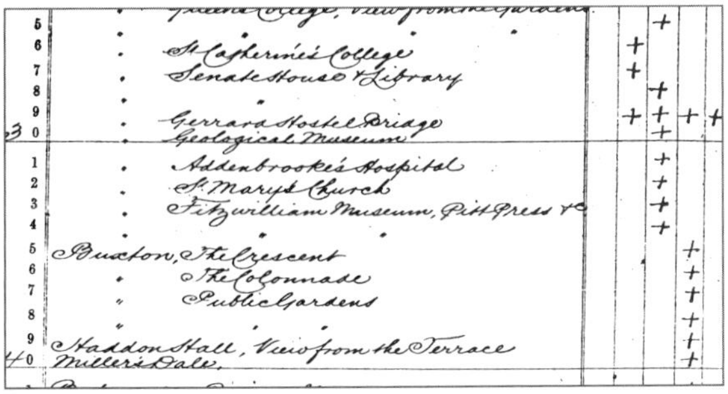
5 . ... College, View from the ...
6 . St Catherine's College
7 . Senate House & Library
8 .
9 .
30 . Gerrard Hostel Bridge
. Geological Museum
1 . Addenbrooke's Hospital
2 . St Mary's Church
3 . Fitzwilliam Museum, Pitt Press &c
4 .
5 Buxton, The Crescent
6 . The Colonnade
7 " Public Gardens
8
9 Haddon Hall, View from the Terrace
40 Miller's Dale

coasts and countryside were opened up to mass travel.

Francis Frith had died in 1898 at his villa in Cannes, his great project still growing. The archive he created continued in business for another seventy years. By 1970 it contained over a third of a million pictures showing 7,000 British towns and villages.

FRANCIS FRITH'S LEGACY

Frith's legacy to us today is of immense significance and value, for the magnificent archive of evocative photographs he created provides a unique record of change in the cities, towns and villages throughout Britain over a century and more. Frith and his fellow studio photographers revisited locations many times down the years to update their views, compiling for us an enthralling and colourful pageant of British life and character.

We are fortunate that Frith was dedicated to recording the minutiae of everyday life. For it is this sheer wealth of visual data, the painstaking chronicle of changes in dress, transport, street layouts, buildings, housing, engineering and landscape that captivates us so much today. His remarkable images offer us a powerful link with the past and with the lives of our ancestors.

THE VALUE OF THE ARCHIVE TODAY

Computers have now made it possible for Frith's many thousands of images to be accessed almost instantly. Frith's images are increasingly used as visual resources, by social historians, by researchers into genealogy and ancestry, by architects and town planners, and by teachers involved in local history projects.

In addition, the archive offers every one of us an opportunity to examine the places where we and our families have lived and worked down the years. Highly successful in Frith's own era, the archive is now, a century and more on, entering a new phase of popularity. Historians consider the Francis Frith Collection to be of prime national importance. It is the only archive of its kind remaining in private ownership. Francis Frith's archive is now housed in an historic timber barn in the beautiful village of Teffont in Wiltshire. Its founder would not recognize the archive office as it is today. In place of the many thousands of dusty boxes containing glass plate negatives and an all-pervading odour of photographic chemicals, there are now ranks of computer screens. He would be amazed to watch his images travelling round the world at unimaginable speeds through internet lines.

The archive's future is both bright and exciting. Francis Frith, with his unshakeable belief in making photographs available to the greatest number of people, would undoubtedly approve of what is being done today with his lifetime's work. His photographs depicting our shared past are now bringing pleasure and enlightenment to millions around the world a century and more after his death.

WIDNES
AND RUNCORN
AN INTRODUCTION

HAD FRANCIS FRITH himself, a little over one hundred years ago, wanted to produce a book of photographs of the towns of Widnes and Runcorn it is highly unlikely that he would have combined them into one volume. Not only did the populations of these two towns see themselves as rivals in just about every way, they were, moreover, even in different counties.

Today, with the formation in 1974 of the single Borough of Halton, Widnes and Runcorn have been united. Considering how inextricably linked these two towns now are and have been in recent years, it is strange to realise that this was not always the case.

It is the bridges over the Runcorn Gap which today bind the two communities so tightly together. But for many centuries it was this same Runcorn Gap which divided them so that the development of both areas was for a long time almost totally separate. Indeed, the River Mersey as it passed between them served as the defining border - the very name 'Mersey' came from Old English 'Maeres-ea' meaning 'boundary river'. At first it was the boundary between the two Saxon kingdoms of Northumbria and Mercia and later, following the unification of these two kingdoms

into a single country called England, the Mersey still served as a border between the two counties of Lancashire and Cheshire.

Besides acting as a boundary the River Mersey was also an important route way, a means of access into the heart of England. It was probably for this reason that in the early 10th century Ethelfleda, Queen of Mercia, built a castle here to protect her realm from Viking attack. This castle would appear to have been extremely effective. It is interesting to note that all along the Wirral there is a preponderance of Viking place names showing us where such raiders must have settled with their families. Yet, behind Ethelfleda's castle at Runcorn there are hardly any such names to be found.

In fact, one of the few Viking names in the region would appear to be that of Widnes itself, sitting on the opposite bank to Ethelfleda's castle. It apparently means 'wide nose' - presumably a reference to the width of land jutting out into the river estuary at this point.

Aside from the fear of Viking raids, this would appear to have been a very pleasant place in which to live in the 10th and 11th centuries. The land was thickly wooded providing good prospects for hunting and interspersed throughout the woodland there would have been small farming communities and along the river banks and sea coasts settlements of fishermen would also have developed.

A thousand years ago Runcorn was still just a small fishing hamlet on the banks of the Mersey whilst Widnes, if it existed at all, probably consisted of little more than one or two small houses.

In fact, if any one settlement would have appeared to dominate the region at that time it would probably have been Frodsham sitting beside the estuary of the nearby River Weaver. It was through here that traders travelled with that vitally important commodity in an age before fridges and freezers - salt from the salt mines of central Cheshire that had been worked since pre-Roman times.

Ethelfleda's castle must have been quite a substantial affair as its remains were discovered when the foundations for the railway bridge were being built beside Runcorn in the 1860s. Following the Norman Conquest of 1066 however,

the Normans were to build a much more substantial castle on higher ground at Halton, overlooking both sides of the estuary.

It was from this later castle that the Baron of Halton was, for the next few hundred years, to control his estates. And these estates extended into both counties of Lancashire and Cheshire so that much of the new, present-day area of the Borough of Halton, on both sides of the Mersey, was contained within the boundaries of the original, ancient borough of Halton. In fact, it was to make it easier for his tenants on the northern banks of the river to pay their dues at the castle that Baron John FitzRichard established the first regular ferry service across the river in 1178.

The Barony of Halton actually still survives. One man who held the title in the late 1300s was John of Gaunt, Duke of Lancaster. He acquired both titles when he married an heiress named Blanche who was the daughter of the 13th Baron of Halton and first Duke of Lancaster. On his own death John of Gaunt's titles passed to his son, Henry Bolinbroke, who subsequently

WIDNES, *Hough Green, Liverpool Road c1965* W97048

became King Henry IV and so the title became one of the hereditary titles of the monarch. To this day in Lancashire the loyal toast takes the form 'The Queen, Duke of Lancaster'.

Aside from the castle at Halton, two settlements now began to develop and take prominence within the area: Runcorn on the south and, on the northern bank of the Mersey, Farnworth. Widnes was still hardly worthy of notice. During the Middle Ages it was Runcorn, however, that developed most and its coastal position meant that it began to grow as a small port serving towns further up the valley of the Mersey to Manchester and beyond.

Runcorn began to be so successful as a port trading, especially, across the Irish Sea that it started to rival the county capital at Chester. Eventually the merchants in that city complained so that the port of Runcorn was forced to end its trading links with Dublin. Runcorn was never to recover. By the time Chester's importance as a port ended it was the ports at Birkenhead and Liverpool that had begun to develop instead.

That is not to say, however, that trading through Runcorn ceased altogether. Also, new industries started to emerge here - industries such as shipbuilding (using timber from the nearby Delamere Forest) and tanneries. This latter industry was to become extremely important in the 1700s and 1800s with the development of factories throughout the Lancashire region, all of which needed endless lengths of leather belting in order for their machines to run smoothly.

And salt still needed to be shipped through both Frodsham and Runcorn. So important was this trade that in the 1700s, and before the building of the first proper canals, the River Weaver was canalised to aid easy transportation of salt to the coastal ports.

And, of course, it was the salt that was to be behind the ultimate development of both Runcorn and Widnes across the river. Strangely, the salt at first served to make Runcorn a spa town with people visiting it for the good of their health. Such were the numbers of visitors that special bath houses were built for bathers on the river's edge near the parish

RUNCORN, *The Railway Viaduct 1900* 45433

church and boarding houses developed within the town.

Meantime, industries dependent on the use of salt also began to develop so that by the mid 1800s the area was already becoming a place to be avoided, rather than visited, if one was concerned for one's health.

It was at this time that Runcorn became a major producer of soap. By 1816 there were already two factories in Runcorn producing soap and turpentine. Another, linked, industry was the production of alkali. An essential ingredient of soap, alkali was also needed in the production of glass and for the finishing of textiles in, for example, Manchester's many cotton mills. By the end of the 19th century the production of alkali was the major industry on both sides of the river.

With the development of these new industries came the development of new towns - at Weston Point on the southern side of the river and at Widnes on the north. The growth was phenomenal - the population of Widnes, for example, doubled every ten years between 1841 and 1871.

But this development came at a terrible cost. The pollution from the chemical industries here was to become the worst in all of Great Britain. It was so severe that at one point the borough of Liverpool sued that of Widnes because of the damage being done by the pollution to trees in Sefton Park. It was no wonder that Widnes, in 1888, was described as 'the dirtiest, ugliest and most depressing town in England'.

Already, in the 1860s and 1870s Alkali Acts had been passed to deal with the problem, but these were having little affect. Nor was the problem entirely self-inflicted - the River Mersey also served as a sewer for all the towns further upstream so that it cannot have been very pleasant living on the banks of the Mersey in either Runcorn or Widnes about 100 years ago.

Even in 1905 a reporter visiting Widnes described the town as a 'poisonous hell-town … a dark, dreadful place of belching, poisonous fumes, defiling and degrading the brightness'.

With the new century came additional new industries based on the chemical expertise that was now well-established here: industries linked

FRODSHAM, *The River Weaver c1965* F176045

to photographic chemicals, insecticides, munitions (including mustard gas), drugs, antiseptics and cosmetics. These new, specialised industries meant that when other industrial centres around this region began to suffer in the years after the Second World War, Widnes and Runcorn were relatively unaffected.

But there were constant problems resulting from the poor system of communications between the two areas because of the lack of an effective bridge for motor vehicles. The opening of the new bridge in 1961 changed all that. It was soon seen to have linked the two communities in ways that no-one would originally have imagined as an increasingly mobile population began to take over more and more land for housing, especially on the southern side of the river.

Some degree of control was required over the inevitable expansion that was taking place, so that in 1964 a new town was proposed in and around Runcorn using green-field sites towards the east and the south. Ten years later, with the introduction of the boundary changes along Cheshire's northern border which brought Widnes into the county, a further decision was made - to unite the two rivals to form one new borough.

This new borough needed a name so, in remembrance of that time some 900 years before when all the lands locally had been part of the barony of Halton, it was decided by a vote of 11 to 2 to call the new town Halton. History often has a strange way of turning full circle! In 1998 this relatively new Borough of Halton was given unitary status so that, although still within the county of Cheshire, it is now independent and is therefore in total control of all its own services.

One hundred years ago people, given the choice, would have preferred to live almost anywhere other than either Widnes or Runcorn. Its reputation as a 'poisonous hell-town' was well deserved and still remains in the mind of many in Britain today. But now the air is clean once more and the trees are flourishing so that in recent years the new Borough of Halton has become an extremely sought-after area in which to live.

FRODSHAM, *Mersey View Pleasure Grounds, Overton Hill c1955* F176036

WIDNES - THE TOWN

WIDNES
*The Technical School and Public Library
1900* 45442

The red-brick and terracotta library and technical school opened in 1896 and had cost £12,976 to build, the land having already been given to the Council in 1878. The first librarian was a lady called Miss Anne Proctor who introduced a system of open access to the books. The library was then only the second one in Lancashire to have such facilities.

WIDNES
*St Paul's Church and
The Free Library 1908*
59503

The library has one of the
largest collections of railway
books of any public library
in Britain - there are around
6,000 books on the subject.
From the beginning it had a
lending department and
reading rooms with a
separate reading room for
ladies. There was no
children's library although
'boys were allowed to read
newspapers in the corridor'.

WIDNES
*The Technical
College c1960*
W97040

Originally Widnes
Technical School, it
gained college status in
1925. The building is
currently undergoing
total renovation so that it
will house not only the
library but also a new
Lifelong Learning Centre
and a coffee shop - this
is due to open in
December 2004.

WIDNES, *The Town Hall 1900* 45444

The Town Hall was built in 1887 in a style described as 'French Renaissance'. The building was used briefly in the 1980s to
house the Halton Chemical Industry Museum. Today Widnes has Europe's only museum dedicated solely to the chemical
industry - it is called Catalyst and occupies the former offices and laboratories of what was once Britain's largest soap
manufacturing firm, Gossages Soaps.

WIDNES
The Town Hall
c1955 W97011

The council offices moved to Kingsway in the 1960s so that the former Town Hall is now home to the Halton Chamber of Commerce. Having always known Widnes and Runcorn as two entirely separate towns it is difficult to become accustomed to the new entity that is called the Borough of Halton. Founded in 1974 it was given unitary status in 1998.

WIDNES, *Victoria Square c1965* W97076

The original intention was that there should be a tower on top of the Town Hall but the local people felt it looked quite grand enough as it was and so did not bother to add it. They saved some money too. This comes as a surprise because Widnesians will tell you it's the folk across the water in Runcorn who are always very careful with their money!

► **WIDNES**
*Town Hall Square
c1965* W97059

This view, from just beside the Town Hall, overlooks what is officially called Victoria Square. The buildings all survive but the whole view has changed considerably with, believe it or not, a much narrower road. Once the heart of the town, modern redevelopment with its open piazzas and places to sit and stroll may look lovely but much of the life has gone from this area.

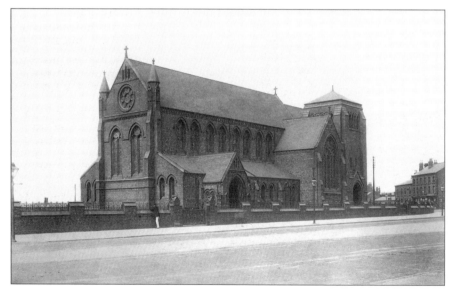

◄**WIDNES**
*St Paul's Church
1900* 45443

The original parish church that served this area was the one at Farnworth that dated from Norman times. Widnes was then just a sleepy little hamlet of a few houses on the banks of the Mersey. With the enormous growth in population here in the 19th century many new churches were needed so St Paul's was built in the 1880s.

▲ WIDNES
Lugsdale Road c1960 W97035

Perhaps this view was taken on a Sunday - notice that the entrances to all the shops on the left have gates closed across them. Sadly, this deserted view gives an early impression of the sense of abandonment that a number of these streets now have permanently - all the main shops that serve the people of Widnes have moved to other parts of town.

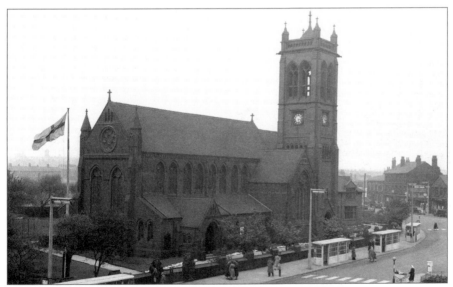

◄ WIDNES
Victoria Square c1955 W97001

Compare this view of St Paul's Church with that in photograph 45443 and you immediately notice the addition of a tall tower which was added in 1907. It's said the original consecration of the church was delayed for three years until all the debts incurred in its construction had been paid.

▼ **WIDNES,** *Municipal Building c1965* W97072

Opened in 1967 and costing £526,495, this building was then considered one of the most modern council offices in England. It overlooks Kingsway, a dual carriageway originally called St Bede's Road. When the route was first laid out it was deemed unlikely that there would ever be much expansion here and it was known locally as 'David Lewis's Folly' after the Councillor who decided on it.

► **WIDNES**
The Technical College c1965
W97074

Just next door to the Municipal Building is the technical college, since renamed Halton College. It was completed in 1961 and now has two campuses for around 1,000 students, one here and one across the river in Runcorn. The grassed area in the foreground in this view has since been taken over by Kingsway when it was widened.

WIDNES
The Swimming Pool c1965
W97075

This swimming pool building was designed by Neville Player, who also designed the College across the road. It opened in 1962 and had a capacity for 220 bathers an hour. It has since been replaced by a new Kingsway Leisure Centre which has, besides a swimming pool, a large sports hall where world championship boxing and premier league snooker matches have taken place.

WIDNES
Widnes Road c1960
W97034

The supermarket is a branch of Tesco. Founded in London in the 1920s, Tesco is now one of the three top retailers in the world, with 1,878 branches in the United Kingdom alone. At the time this photograph was taken the company was expanding rapidly but no-one could have imagined then just how it would grow. Today this building (with an additional floor) is a Kwiksave supermarket.

WIDNES
Widnes Road c1960
W97031

This view was taken in Albert Road looking down Widnes Road. Today the whole focus of the shopping centre of Widnes has moved from the area around Victoria Square about a mile away so that it is now centred here and the street has become a pedestrian area with many of the major shops and banks established here.

▼ WIDNES, *Widnes Road c1960* W97032

Notice the ornate sign outside Neil and Barker's shop. The three balls, the sign of a pawnbroker, are said to originate from St Nicholas, the patron saint of pawnbrokers. They represent the bags of gold that he once gave to three girls to save them from destitution. St Nicholas, of course, is usually better known these days as Santa Claus.

► WIDNES
St Bede's Roman Catholic Church 1900
45445

St Bede's Church, built in 1847, is situated in an area once known as Appleton. It was so-called because of all the apple orchards here - in fact it was said that on one day alone eight tons of apples were once picked here to be sent to market in Liverpool.

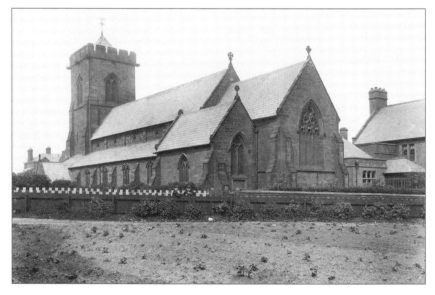

◄ **WIDNES**
*The Park Entrance
1900* 45446

Established on 34 acres of land that had previously belonged to the Appleton House estate, Victoria Park opened to the public in 1900. The gates shown here were donated by Widnes Foundry and actually date from 1897.

► **WIDNES**
Victoria Park c1955
W97014

The fountain in the foreground was dedicated in 1903 to the former Prime Minister, William Gladstone. Beyond it can be seen Widnes's war memorial which lists 818 men from the town who died in the First World War, the youngest a boy aged only 15. A further 289 names were added after the Second World War. The plinth on which the column stands is 7ft high and the obelisk is 42ft with a sculpted eternal flame at the top.

WIDNES - THE SUBURBS

FARNWORTH, *The Church 1900* 45446A

Once the most important village of many around Widnes, Farnworth is now merely a small suburb of the larger town. The first church on this site was founded about 1180 and was dedicated to St Wilfrid. The church we see today, however, was rebuilt in the 1800s at which time it was rededicated to St Luke. Church registers here date back to 1538 and one early name is that of Richard Bancroft who grew up to become Archbishop of Canterbury (he died in 1611).

FARNWORTH
The Church and Cottage 1900 45446B

Not surprisingly this little cottage has since been demolished. It was in Farnworth that the Farnworth and Appleton Football Club was formed in 1873. Two years afterwards it was renamed Widnes Football Club and is now better known as Widnes Rugby League Football Club or, to the locals, as 'the Vikings'.

WIDNES, *Ball o'Ditton, Liverpool Road c1965* W97057

There was once a pub in this area which was called the Ball which may be where the name Ball o' Ditton comes from. All along Liverpool Road, and to both sides of it, there was tremendous development from the mid 1800s in response to the need to accommodate people coming to work in the new chemical industries in both Widnes and Runcorn. These workers came from far and near - from Wales and Ireland and from Poland and Lithuania!

▲ WIDNES
Ball O' Ditton,
Bankfield School
c1965 W97056

Local growth was
particularly strong in the
years after the Second
World War with around
5,000 houses built by the
early 1970s in this area
alone. New schools were
therefore needed and,
today, Bankfield School
has around 900 pupils
aged between 11 and 16.
Due to the importance of
local chemical and related
industries the school has
a strong technology and
science department.

▶ *detail from W97056*

WIDNES
Hough Green, Liverpool Road
c1965 W97048

The name 'Hough' anywhere in the Cheshire region tends to indicate a settlement that was on a slight ridge or spur of land. It's difficult, as you drive along Liverpool Road, to distinguish any ridge here today but with the lowlands of the Mersey estuary nearby any slight ridge overlooking that valley would have been settled very early in history.

DITTON, *Ditchfield Road c1965* D708049

Any early farmstead close to the coast would have been an easy target for raiders and so probably needed defensive ditches - 'Ditton' means a farmstead with a ditch or dyke nearby. The name also survived through the centuries in 'Ditchfield' Hall which gave this road its name in the 19th century.

► **DITTON**
Ditchfield Road
c1965 D708052

There have
been several
Ditchfield Halls near
here. In the 1500s
and 1600s the
Dychfield family
that lived here were
strong Roman
Catholics and
refused to attend the
Protestant services
at their local parish
church at
Farnworth. Instead
they built their own
chapel but they were
still fined for not
attending the official
church services! The
last Ditchfield Hall
was demolished in
the 1960s.

◀ **DITTON**
*St Michael's Church
c1965* D708050

With so many workers arriving here in the 1800s from Ireland there was a strong Roman Catholic presence and this enormous church was built in the 1870s to serve that congregation. For the first 23 years it was also a collegiate church for Jesuits with, at one time, 32 priests, 22 scholastics and 17 lay brothers.

THE RIVER
MERSEY AND
ITS BRIDGES

WIDNES, *West Bank 1923* 73918

When Widnes Town Council decided to buy land to establish Victoria Park to the north of the town, some of the money was put aside in order to develop a promenade overlooking the waterfront and this is still a pleasant place to walk today. In this view the buildings in front of the church have all been replaced in recent years. Notice especially the group on The Promenade - they have two cameras on tripods with them, presumably to photograph the Transporter Bridge.

WIDNES, *The Promenade 1923* 73917

It would have been near here that the ferry landed. The first ferry was established in 1178 by the baron who owned Halton Castle on the southern side of the estuary. His estates included lands on the northern side and, apparently, the ferry was set up primarily so his tenants could cross the river more easily in order to pay him their taxes.

▶ **WIDNES**
*Church Gardens
1923* 73919

St Mary's Church was consecrated in 1910 and has room for a congregation of over 750 people. The church has a most unusual feature - built into the wall around the churchyard, overlooking the road, there is a pulpit from where, perhaps, the vicar could harangue those people taking their ease here in the gardens on a Sunday afternoon.

◀ **RUNCORN**
*The Railway Viaduct
1900* 45433

When digging foundations for the footings on the far side of the railway bridge the Victorian engineers discovered the remains of a Saxon fortification built in AD 915 by Queen Ethelfleda. As a result local people have always called this bridge the Ethelfleda Bridge. But it has two 'official' names, sometimes it is called the Widnes-Runcorn Railway Bridge and sometimes the Britannia Railway Bridge.

▲ **WIDNES**
The Bridge c1965 W97062

Despite the title of the photograph there are, in fact, two bridges depicted here. The railway bridge, in the foreground, was opened in 1868 when a train with 500 passengers on board crossed over. The main part of the bridge consists of a lattice of iron girders. Built by William Baker, the chief engineer for the London and North Western Railway, it used 48,115 rivets.

◄ **RUNCORN**
The Transporter Bridge c1906 43432A

The Transporter (or more correctly 'transbordeur') Bridge was a meccano-like structure below which moved a suspended cab. It was built by John James Webster who was born in Warrington and was later to build the Shepherd's Bush Stadium in London for the Olympic Games of 1908. The bridge was opened in May 1905 and with a span of 1,000ft it was then the longest vehicular bridge in Britain.

RUNCORN
The Transporter Bridge c1920 R67302

The height of the bridge was required so that ships could pass underneath. In this photograph, however, we see a rather small ship - it's one of the 'Mersey Flats'. These were local boats built with a strong hull so they could sit on the mud at low tide, even with a full cargo on board. This style of boat was used not only on the Mersey but also along the River Weaver where they carried salt from Northwich.

WIDNES, *The Transporter Bridge c1955* W97016

The towers of the bridge were 150ft high and at the top of each there was a lantern with a copper roof. Following the demolition of the bridge one of these lanterns is said to have been briefly used as a sweet shop on the road to Chester. Notice the queue of cars waiting to cross over - the bridge became so busy that on summer weekends in the 1950s it wasn't unknown to have to wait two hours in the queue here.

▲ **RUNCORN**
The Transporter Bridge
c1955 R67035

The car carrying vehicles and foot passengers usually took up to four minutes to cross from one side to the other. It was 55 ft long, 24ft wide and could carry 300 passengers and, to begin with, four two-horse wagons. There were numerous tolls (it cost 5d for an adult corpse to cross the bridge!). On the Widnes side of the bridge the world's first double-decker bus service was started in 1909 especially to meet passengers from the bridge and give them a ride into the centre of the town.

◀ *detail from R67035*

▲ **WIDNES**
The Transporter Bridge c1955 W97003

Notice the chimney on the left doing its best to improve the air quality of Widnes. In fact the air quality here was so atrocious there was great concern about its affect on the bridge's iron frame. To counteract this all the cables used in the structure were coated with bitumen and then wrapped in sail-cloth which had itself also been saturated in bitumen.

▶ *detail from W97003*

WIDNES, *The Transporter Bridge c1955* W97009

The bust on the plinth in the foreground is of Creighton Hutchinson, a local doctor and benefactor, who died in 1927. The last crossing of the Transporter Bridge took place on 22 July 1961 (the day after the new bridge was opened) with 250 specially invited guests going along for the ride.

◄ **WIDNES**
The Bridges 1961
W97017

This is an interesting photograph showing all three bridges crossing the Runcorn Gap. Even now there are plans for another bridge which would probably cost around £123 million. Notice the people on the railway bridge footpath. This path was closed in the 1960s but before closure it was used by around 1,000 people each day, many of whom were cyclists. Pedestrians paid 1d to cross the bridge.

◄ **RUNCORN**, *Widnes Bridge 1961* R67043

No sooner had the new bridge opened than the old one was closed and demolished. Apparently it cost £2,000 more to demolish the bridge in 1961 than it had to build it in 1905. It is interesting to compare this photograph with another taken a few years later (R67049 below) after the Transporter Bridge had been demolished.

◄ **RUNCORN**
Widnes Bridge
c1965 R67049

The effect of the new bridge on housing nearby can be seen in this photograph. Demolition of houses along the route of the approach roads began in 1956 so that although the bridge itself cost £3 million, the approach roads added a further £1.5 million to the bill.

WIDNES, *Runcorn-Widnes Bridge 1961* W97018

The bridge was opened by Princess Alexandra on 21 July 1961. More than 5,000 tons of steel was used in its construction. If the curve of the bridge looks familiar it may be because it reminds you of the Sydney Harbour Bridge which was built by the same company, Dorman Long, who also built the Forth Road Bridge, the Severn Bridge and the Humber Bridge.

WIDNES
High Level Road Bridge c1965
W97067

To give the bridge just one coat of paint requires 6,000 gallons of paint. Today the maintenance of the bridge and its approach roads consume about a third of Halton's entire highways budget. The cost isn't helped by the fact that each winter around half a million starlings roost on the bridge!

RUNCORN, *The Bridge c1965* R67361

Within 15 years of being built the bridge needed to be widened so that today it carries four lanes of traffic. When this work was completed in 1977 (at a cost of £12 million) the bridge was renamed the Silver Jubilee Bridge in honour of the Queen's Jubilee that same year - a most appropriate name as it glistens like silver when the sun shines on it. It also solves the problem of deciding what to call it - just in the titles of these photographs there is a plethora of other names being used.

RUNCORN'S CANALS AND DOCKS

RUNCORN, *The Two Bridges 1929* 82384

In this view from the south side of the River Mersey, the expanse of water just beyond the road is the Manchester Ship Canal. Notice the height of both the railway and transporter bridges - required for the masts of the ships passing below. It was perhaps just as well that Thomas Telford's plans in the early 1800s for a suspension bridge at this point never materialised as it would have had to have been demolished anyway when the canal was built.

RUNCORN
The Two Bridges c1955
R67032

Runcorn's port had had a chequered history from the 1400s when merchants in Chester complained at the 'unfair' competition resulting in Runcorn being banned from trading with Dublin. It later became a creek port serving Liverpool where there was a customs office. For a short time in the mid 1800s Runcorn was briefly independent with its own customs office, but then, following the opening of the Manchester Ship Canal, it came under the authority of the city of Manchester.

RUNCORN, *The Swing Bridge and Canal 1900* 45435

The Old Quay Swing Bridge opens by pivoting on the pier on the left hand side of the canal. The Manchester Ship Canal has been described as 'the greatest civil engineering project of the Victorian Age'. It was opened by Queen Victoria in 1894 and could carry the largest ocean-going vessels of the day. In its first six months of operation 630 sea-going vessels passed along it.

RUNCORN
The Old Quay 1929
82386

Another view of the
Manchester Ship Canal, in
this case beside the Old
Quay. Today this area has
totally changed with private
houses where there was
once docks all along the
canalside - it must be a
weird sensation to see great
ocean-going liners sail past
your living room window!

RUNCORN
The Docks c1900
R67301

This view shows the docks at Weston Point. The enormous piles of white stone are actually piles of china clay from Cornwall awaiting trans-shipment onto narrow boats so they can be taken to the china factories in Stoke-on-Trent. Later the finished article would be exported through here - in 1883 alone 50,000 tons of china goods were exported through this port.

RUNCORN
Weston 1929 82379

It is difficult looking at this view to imagine that it was ever once covered in woodland with small fisheries along the shore. It is a far cry, too, from the Runcorn that was described in 1834 as 'celebrated for its situation, being surrounded by a beautifully romantic and picturesque scenery' where, according to another visitor in 1795, 'lovers of botany may find a pleasing variety of plants'.

RUNCORN, *Weston Point c1955* R67019

It was the production of soap and alkali that became the most important industry here resulting from the proximity of salt from Cheshire and coal from Lancashire. Alkali was needed not only for the production of soap but also to finish textiles in the nearby Lancashire cotton mills. It was produced using salt mixed with sulphuric acid; this was treated to produce soda crystals which were then converted into caustic soda or alkali. The conditions in which it was produced were horrendous and the pollution it caused was worse than anywhere else in Britain.

FRODSHAM
The River Weaver
c1965 F176045

This peaceful view of the River Weaver belies its earlier importance. This was an essential route bringing salt from inland Cheshire to the coast, so important, in fact, that the river was canalised in the early 1700s. The estuary of the River Weaver, close to Frodsham, also became an important ship-building area.

RUNCORN, *The Hill 1923* 73911

In the 1800s this area was one vast quarry. Stone from here was used to build the docks at Liverpool, Holker Hall in Cumbria and Tatton Hall in nearby Knutsford. It is even said that it was used for the building of the docks in New York, the stone originally travelling there as ballast in sailing ships. The stone was also particularly good for the sharpening of tools so that it was exported for this purpose to tool manufacturers all around the world.

▶ **RUNCORN**
The Hill 1923
73909

By the 1900s the best stone had been worked out from the area so in the 1920s it was laid out as parkland. Notice the flat area in the mid-right-hand side - this was intended as a platform on which concerts were to be held. Today, however, the valley is thickly wooded and it would be impossible to hold a concert here. Instead the hill is now an important nature reserve.

◀ **RUNCORN**
Weston Road 1923 73913

Runcorn Hill, with all its quarries, is on the left. In the distance it's possible to see the industrial area of Weston Point. Much of the stone from the quarries used to be taken to Weston along linking tunnels which pass beneath Weston Road. These were later to be used as air-raid shelters during the Second World War.

▲ RUNCORN
Weston Cross c1960 R67022

The old village of Weston, sitting on Runcorn Hill, has given its name to Weston Point where the docks and industries are largely to be found. This ancient preaching cross has been restored more than once so that today only the plinth is original. It is thought that it may have been used for preachers in open-air religious meetings at the time of the Reformation.

◄ RUNCORN
Weston Church and Village c1960 R67023

Weston's church, dedicated to St John the Evangelist, was built in the 1890s using money entirely raised from donations. Nearby is the village hall. Built to serve as a school for the children of workers who came into the region to work on the Manchester Ship Canal, it was closed in 1902 after the canal was completed and these families all followed their work elsewhere.

▶ **RUNCORN**
The Locks
c1955 R67002

There were ten locks at the end of the Bridgewater Canal linking it with the docks below; figures for 1883 show that in that year alone 60,300 craft passed up and down. The bridge shown here is the railway bridge. Soon after this photograph was taken the canal at this point (and in picture R67003) was filled in prior to the building of the new bridge.

◄ RUNCORN
The Locks c1955 R67003

The Bridgewater Canal was the first proper canal to be built and it linked Manchester with Worsley. It was so successful that an extension was then dug to the port at Runcorn. It was financed by the Duke of Bridgewater and built by James Brindley. In fact Brindley wanted to take it all the way to Liverpool using an aqueduct over the Runcorn Gap but could not raise the financial backing to do so. Notice the two men on the towpath pulling the barges.

▶ RUNCORN
Top Locks c1955 R67001

The Bridgewater Canal was
built solely for the
transportation of freight but
so many people came to see
it that a passenger service
was soon started between
Warrington and Manchester.
This service was so
profitable that it was soon
extended to Runcorn - the
journey from Top Locks to
Manchester took about
eight hours. Meals were
served during the journey by
a stewardess on board the
narrowboat.

◄ **RUNCORN**
The Basin c1965 R67079

Compare this photograph with R67001 - the new bridge carries one of the approach roads to the Jubilee Bridge. Today the canal comes to an end near here. Evidence of the docks has nearly all gone and trees have been planted. There are still boats but these are now holiday craft from all over the country. In 1882 there were 823 canal boats registered in Runcorn.

THE OLD TOWN OF RUNCORN

RUNCORN
All Saints' Church 1894 33811

The Manchester Ship Canal runs just behind the church. The church, large enough to hold over 1,000 people, was built in the 1840s at a cost of £8,052. It was designed by Anthony Salvin and built using stone from the nearby Runcorn Hill quarries.

▲ **RUNCORN**
All Saints' Church
1900 45438

Just to the left of All Saints'
Church the Railway Bridge
can be clearly seen
standing where Queen
Ethelfleda's castle was built
to control and watch the
Runcorn Gap and protect
her kingdom of Mercia.
The first church on this site
is also said to have been
founded by Ethelfleda at
the same time, in AD915.
That first church was
dedicated to a Mercian
prince called St Bertelin.

◄ *detail from 45438*

63

RUNCORN, *The Parish Church c1965* R67055

Notice that all the tombstones have disappeared. In fact they have been laid flat on the ground and used for footpaths all around the church. In view of the acidity of the air here from all the industrial pollution it is remarkable to discover that many of the tombstones are still in excellent condition with inscriptions that are very easy to read.

RUNCORN
The Church Interior 1894
33813

The first Saxon church here was replaced by a church built by the Normans, probably about 1250. That church was dedicated to St Bartholemew. Prior to its demolition in the 1840s a new organ had been installed in 1827 and it is this organ that can be seen at the end of the north aisle of the new church.

RUNCORN, *St Paul's Church 1900* 45437

Another fine church, St Paul's was opened in 1866 for the local Methodist congregation. It cost £8,000 and all of this money was paid by one benefactor, Thomas Hazelhurst. Hazelhurst was a soap manufacturer who was wealthy in his own right and then inherited additional money when his wife died, money that he used to build churches, chapels and schools throughout the area.

▲ **RUNCORN,** *Devonshire Place c1960* R67044

With the removal of both the main shopping and administrative areas of Runcorn some miles away these photographs show a town that, in the last 40 years, has changed enormously. Devonshire Place takes its name from the building on the left just beyond the crossroads called the Devonshire Buildings. Notice the Transporter Bridge in the background.

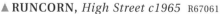

▲ **RUNCORN,** *High Street c1965* R67061

The buildings on the corner here date from the 1860s. Notice the white building on the left with the fine windows. In the 1960s it was home to a branch of the Runcorn and Widnes Industrial Co-Operative Society. The Co-Operative movement began just over the Mersey, in Lancashire, in the 1840s and rapidly spread throughout the industrial heartlands of northern England.

▲ **RUNCORN**
St Paul's Church c1965 R67063

Unfortunately St Paul's Church was demolished in 1969 (just over 100 years after it had been built). Nikolaus Pevsner said of its demolition that Runcorn had thereby 'lost its one distinctive building'. Incidentally, the church was renowned for its acoustics and was used for many concerts - Kathleen Ferrier once sang here during the Second World War.

▶ **RUNCORN**
*The Town Centre
c1965* R67062

Runcorn grew rapidly in the early 1800s from a town in 1801 with a population of just under 1,500 to one with over 10,000 people only 30 years later. However, by the beginning of the 1960s, just before the act that designated the area as a new town, the population had only grown to over 26,000 people.

◄ **RUNCORN**
Church Street c1965
R67068

This slow growth of population in the 1900s is explained by the fact that Runcorn was very much a cul-de-sac town. Although the Transporter Bridge had opened in 1905 vehicular crossing wasn't easy and the presence of the bridge did not, at that time, encourage growth within the town.
It was said of Runcorn that it was 'like the Dead Sea - there's a road into it but none out'. It was the building of the new bridge that really encouraged development locally.

RUNCORN
Church Street c1965
R67071

It may not seem so from these photographs, but Church Street has always been, and is still, a relatively busy part of the old town area despite the fact that the main shops have moved elsewhere. Nikolaus Pevsner obviously didn't care much for Runcorn - he said in 1971, 'Runcorn is miserable to look at, so the best of luck to the new Runcorn'.

RUNCORN, *Church Street c1965* R67067

There's a sign on the building on the left that reads 'National Health Dispensing Service'. Believe it or not Runcorn in the 1790s was considered an excellent place to visit for the good of your health and it was said of it that 'the air is impregnated with health (and) the salt bathing is very good'. But with the coming of industrialisation this attraction soon disappeared.

RUNCORN
The Market Hall
c1965 R67066

When this market hall was built a number of houses, shops and even a church were demolished to make way for it. There has been a great deal of concern locally following the severe decline of old Runcorn that resulted from all the investment in

the new town development around Halton Lea. Today this market has also gone but the site is now part of a new local multi-million pound regeneration scheme. It is planned that the new market hall will open in September 2004.

RUNCORN, *Big Pool 1923* 73906

Once linked to the Bridgewater Canal, this view was taken near to Heath Road. The pool was subsequently drained and filled in prior to the development of the later road system around Runcorn. Today the Daresbury Expressway literally flies overhead.

RUNCORN'S SUBURBS

RUNCORN
Greenway Road from the Memorial c1955
R67010

Those people who could afford it were, already in the 1800s, establishing their homes beyond the old town of Runcorn on the higher ground around Runcorn Hill. But even here there was then a constant cloud of polluted air. Today, thanks to all the Clean Air Acts that have since taken effect, this is now a delightful suburb of the town.

RUNCORN
The War Memorial 1923
73916

At the top of Greenway Road, looking back towards the heart of old Runcorn is the war memorial. It was unveiled in November 1920 and listed 400 local men who died in the First World War - of the 2,000 men from Runcorn who served in that war, around one in every five died. It's good also to see that the names of those killed in the service of our country today are still being added to this memorial.

RUNCORN, *The Cemetery 1894* 33814

Opened in 1860 on what was then the edge of the town, Runcorn's cemetery was to replace the graveyard around All Saints' Church. It covers an area of 13 acres. The two chapels pictured here have recently been demolished - one of the chapels was for the use of members of the Church of England and the other was for Dissenters.

▼ **RUNCORN**
The Cottage Hospital 1923 73915

Known locally as the Cottage Hospital (its real name was the Victoria Memorial Hospital) the hospital was opened in 1903. It was designed by James Wilding, a Liverpool man who was associated with a number of buildings in the town and who also played an important part in the development of Runcorn Hill as a park once the quarries there had been closed down.

► **HIGHER RUNCORN**
Highlands Road Bowling Green c1955 R67016

The open parkland of Runcorn Hill also included areas for more organised games and activities. The charge to use the bowling green in 1928 was 3d per person per session. To use the nearby tennis courts also cost 3d each if you were playing doubles or 6d per person for a singles game.

HIGHER RUNCORN
Highlands Road c1955
R67018

Leading to Runcorn Hill, Highlands Road and the surrounding area is a lovely part of the town. Of the cottages shown here only the one in the foreground still survives. Many of these houses were originally built in the 1800s as housing for immigrants coming to the area from Cumbria and North Wales to work in the local quarries.

▶ HIGHER RUNCORN
Highlands Road c1955 R67017

It's said that this street was once known as 'Snuffy Row' because so many quarrymen who lived here had a strong liking for snuff. In a document dated 1295 this area was referred to as 'Runcoure Superior' - this had nothing to do with the class of people who lived here but referred to the fact that it was on the hill; it's still known as Higher Runcorn.

▶ **RUNCORN**
The Town Hall
c1955 R67012

This delightful house, originally known as Halton Grange, was built by the soap manufacturer, Thomas Johnson in the 1850s. It was designed to emulate Queen Victoria's home on the Isle of Wight, Osborne House. Bought by the Council in the 1930s it was then converted for use as a Town Hall.

◀ **RUNCORN**
The Public Hall c1965
R67075

The opening of the bridge over the Runcorn Gap in 1961 meant that Runcorn was now an attractive and easily accessible place to live for those people who worked on the northern side of the River Mersey. Soon afterwards, therefore, a decision was taken, in 1964, to develop Runcorn as a New Town and this led to immediate growth of the town with the corresponding development of new municipal buildings such as the one shown here, just behind the Town Hall.

▲ **RUNCORN,** *Town Hall Gardens c1955* R67009

When Halton Grange was bought by the Council the purchase included the grounds around it which extended to 12 acres. In fact there was a public outcry in the town at the time at the expense of the purchase - it cost £2,250. It has to be remembered that this was a period of severe economic depression throughout the country.

◀ **RUNCORN**
Feeding the Animals 1929 82394

This delightful picture reminds us of what was lost with the development of Runcorn. Following the New Towns Act of 1964, 37 farms and 7,500 acres of land were taken over and absorbed as the new town developed. Perhaps this cottage still survives but I am sure there will no longer be calves, pigs and chickens in the yard.

BEYOND
RUNCORN

HALTON
The Castle 1900 45440

It's amazing to think that Halton is now the centre of the modern town once more; history has turned full circle. If only as an important viewpoint, the site was bound to have been used by the Romans and Saxons. It was certainly used by the Normans who built a castle from where the Baron of Halton could control the Mersey estuary and surrounding lands.

HALTON
The Castle 1900
45439

The large building to the right of the castle is St Mary's Church with its little bell-turret looking very much like an afterthought. The church was designed by Sir George Gilbert Scott and built in 1852 using local Runcorn stone. Just behind the church there is a small building that was built to house one of the country's first public lending libraries as long ago as 1733.

HALTON, *Castle Ruins 1894* 33815

During the Civil War in the 1600s Halton Castle was besieged and subsequently 'slighted' - in other words it was damaged to such an extent that it could not be refortified. The gatehouse survived, however, and was still being used as a prison in the 1700s. Today there is a pub called the Castle that sits on the site.

▶ **MOORE**
The School c1955
M240012

Moore is so called because this was once very boggy land close to the river. In fact the peat around the village used to be dug by the local people for use as fuel. They were not, however, allowed to dig it for sale - presumably this was a way of controlling the amount that was cut each year. The school pictured here was built in 1878 but is no longer used as a school.

◀ **MOORE**
The Canal Bridge c1955 M240008

Today the land around here has been drained and is now excellent farming land. This drainage took place when the canals were being cut so that the village sits between two canals (the Bridgewater and the Manchester Ship Canal). This view shows the Bridgewater Canal. Today the heart of the village is a conservation area.

▲ DARESBURY
The Parish Church c1955 D151001

A stained glass window in Daresbury's church depicts characters from the stories of Alice in Wonderland. This is because it was in this church that Charles Lutwidge Dodgeson, better known to most of us as Lewis Carroll, was baptised in 1832. His father was the vicar here and Dodgeson was born in the nearby vicarage, which has since burnt down.

◄ DUTTON
The Hospital c1955
D263011

This 'commodious and handsome' building has now gone. Costing £7,500, it was built in 1857 as a workhouse for over 200 'destitute and aged folk' with a master and matron who had to be man and wife and whose salary was £80 per annum 'with rations'. It subsequently became an isolation hospital (when Runcorn's isolation hospital was closed in 1939) and ended its days as a geriatric home.

▶ **DUTTON**
The Village
c1960 D263001

The Talbot Arms pub on the right hand side of the photograph has now been renamed the Tunnel Top because there is an air vent nearby for the canal tunnel that runs under the present-day road. A new estate of housing also now replaces the post office and shop on the left so that this view is very much altered.

◄ **DUTTON**
The Canal c1960
D263007

The Trent and Mersey Canal was completed in 1777. Like the Bridgewater Canal it was built by James Brindley and it linked with the Bridgewater at Runcorn - the two canals meet within another tunnel, yet further reminding us of the complexity of the engineering required to build even the earliest canals.

◀ **FRODSHAM**
Mersey View Pleasure Grounds, Overton Hill c1955 F176036

Although not within the present-day borough of Halton, Frodsham has always been closely linked with the district. The building of the railway in the 1800s brought people here for amusement and, before long, the pleasure grounds were established. Today these have gone, but people still come here for entertainment as there is now a hotel with a leisure complex and nightclub on the site.

◄ **ASTON**
The Church
c1955 A360002

Difficult though it is to believe when you see it, this delightful little church was restored in 1950 having been badly damaged by bombs during an air raid in 1940. Originally a chapel of ease within the much larger parish of Runcorn it became a separate parish church in 1861.

◄ **FRODSHAM**
Overton Church
c1965 F176023

Described once as 'a magnificent little cathedral' there has been a church on this site since at least the 11th century. The present St Laurence's church dates from the 12th century but was restored and partly rebuilt in the 1880s. Frodsham's war memorial, seen here in the foreground, has since been moved into the churchyard and the open area turned into a car park.

FRODSHAM
From the Hill c1955
F176009

It could almost be said that there are two Frodshams, one settlement that nestles just under Overton Hill and a second that developed along Main and High Streets. St Laurence's Church is just below the hill and the steeple of Trinity Methodist Church in the distance indicates the position of High Street.

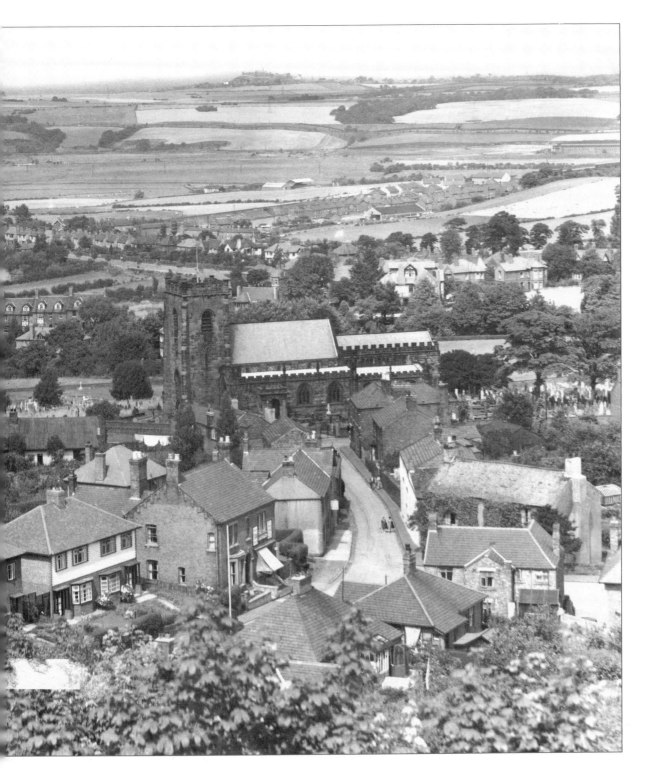

▲ FRODSHAM
High Street c1955
F176019

Through the centuries the most important part of Frodsham was High Street, thanks to the weekly market held here from the 11th century. Stagecoaches regularly passed through so that the Bear's Paw Inn (on the left) was built in 1632 to serve this trade. It still survives although, for about 50 years, it was renamed the Bear's Paw and Railway Hotel after the railway was built.

▶ *detail from F176019*

INDEX

NAMES OF SUBSCRIBERS

The following people have kindly supported this book by subscribing to copies before publication.

Thomas Tyrrell Atkinson, Chester

The Bailes Family, Runcorn

Mr & Mrs I Bailey, Widnes 9-7-2005

Ian McBain Bantang

Jean & Ted Barber

The Barber Family, Widnes

Jean Beckett & Eddie Charnock, Runcorn

Edith Bellfield, Runcorn

Alma & Eric Bradbury, Runcorn

Glenn Briggs, Runcorn

William B Caddick

Peter Coleman, Runcorn

Mr H Shepherd Cook & Mrs Ruth M Cook

In memory of Harold & Betty Cooper

In memory of the Crompton Family

The Daley Family, Runcorn

C W Darlington, Runcorn

E M Davies, Runcorn

Mr G & Mrs L Davies of Widnes

Val Day, Goat Lover & Protector, Cyprus

The Dooley Family, Widnes

The Dutton Family, Runcorn

Reg & Kath Dutton, Runcorn

The Fay Family, Runcorn

The France & Jones Families, Runcorn

Mr G & Mrs G E Fryer, Runcorn

Frank Gandy, Widnes

Brenda May & Donald Garnett of Widnes

Tommy Glynn, Henderson Road

Stephen Gregory of Runcorn

Brian R Griffiths, Runcorn

The Halfpenny Family, Widnes 2004

The Hallwood Family, Widnes & Runcorn

Mr J A & Mrs H M Haydock, Widnes

Mrs Carole Higgins, Mark & Philip

Mrs Pauline J Hurst, Widnes

Mr D O Hutchinson

The Ireland family, Runcorn

Mr Brian N Janion, Runcorn

To John, love from Mum & Dad, Christmas 2004

Philip John, Littlemore

In memory of R Johnson

In memory of Eric Jones, Widnes

Gareth & Gemma Jones, Runcorn 2004

Neil Jones, Runcorn 2004

Mr P R Jones & Mrs S Jones, Widnes

Mr R & Mrs A Jones, Widnes

Brian, Sue, Tony & Josh Kelly, Bilton Close

Dennis & Eileen Kelly, Avondale Drive

Mr R G & Mrs M Knight

Mr H & Mrs H Leach & Children, Widnes

Gwynneth Lowe, Runcorn

Celebrating 50 years of Lunt's Pharmacy

Mr R & Mrs M L Lyon

In memory of Derrick James McCann, Runcorn

Alan Mercer

Mr John Bryan Murray

In memory of Bob & Mary Neale

T P O'Connor, Widnes

Tim O'Dwyer

In memory of Liam J O'Neill, Widnes

Mr K & Mrs M Pearsall, Runcorn

Joyce & Roy Pickering

In memory of Iris Potter, Widnes

Pat Preston, Widnes

C R Price, Widnes

K A Price, Chorlton, Manchester

Duncan Prince, Runcorn

Mr T R & Mrs P Rathbone, Runcorn

Leslie Raven

Kay Rigby (nee Whitfield)

The Rowlinson Family, Runcorn

Alan Ryder, Runcorn

Carole Anne Seel, Runcorn

John Shallcross, Runcorn

In memory of Mrs P Shaw, Widnes

Rodney Shaw

The Sheldon Family, Runcorn

J E Stringer, Runcorn

Marjorie Strong on her Birthday 30-11-04

M Sutton, Widnes

Mr T W Temple & Family, Widnes

The Townley Family

The Truscott Family & The Hitchen Family

In memory of Hugh Turner, Widnes

Mr William Turton, Ms Veronica Mitchell

Jimmy Twigg

Mr Wap & Mrs L Ledward, Runcorn

Mrs Olwen Wardall, Runcorn

John Webb, Widnes

E J Whimperley

Frederick Whinterley

To Bert Wilde, Widnes, 'Happy Birthday'

Linda D Wilding, Runcorn

In memory of Harold Winstanley, Widnes

James W Yates

FRITH PRODUCTS & SERVICES

Francis Frith would doubtless be pleased to know that the pioneering publishing venture he started in 1860 still continues today. Over a hundred and forty years later, The Francis Frith Collection continues in the same innovative tradition and is now one of the foremost publishers of vintage photographs in the world. Some of the current activities include:

Interior Decoration

Today Frith's photographs can be seen framed and as giant wall murals in thousands of pubs, restaurants, hotels, banks, retail stores and other public buildings throughout the country. In every case they enhance the unique local atmosphere of the places they depict and provide reminders of gentler days in an increasingly busy and frenetic world.

Product Promotions

Frith products are used by many major companies to promote the sales of their own products or to reinforce their own history and heritage. Frith promotions have been used by Hovis bread, Courage beers, Scots Porage Oats, Colman's mustard, Cadbury's foods, Mellow Birds coffee, Dunhill pipe tobacco, Guinness, and Bulmer's Cider.

Genealogy and Family History

As the interest in family history and roots grows world-wide, more and more people are turning to Frith's photographs of Great Britain for images of the towns, villages and streets where their ancestors lived; and, of course, photographs of the churches and chapels where their ancestors were christened, married and buried are an essential part of every genealogy tree and family album.

Frith Products

All Frith photographs are available Framed or just as Mounted Prints and Posters (size 23 x 16 inches). These may be ordered from the address below. From time to time other products - Address Books, Calendars, Table Mats, etc - are available.

The Internet

Already fifty thousand Frith photographs can be viewed and purchased on the internet through the Frith websites and a myriad of partner sites.

For more detailed information on Frith companies and products, look at these sites:

www.francisfrith.co.uk
www.francisfrith.com
(for North American visitors)

See the complete list of Frith Books at:

www.francisfrith.co.uk

This web site is regularly updated with the latest list of publications from the Frith Book Company. If you wish to buy books relating to another part of the country that your local bookshop does not stock, you may purchase on-line.

For further information, trade, or author enquiries please contact us at the address below:
The Francis Frith Collection, Frith's Barn, Teffont, Salisbury, Wiltshire, England SP3 5QP.
Tel: +44 (0)1722 716 376 Fax: +44 (0)1722 716 881   Email: sales@francisfrith.co.uk

See Frith books on the internet at www.francisfrith.co.uk

FREE PRINT OF YOUR CHOICE

Mounted Print
Overall size 14 x 11 inches (355 x 280mm)

Choose any Frith photograph in this book.
Simply complete the Voucher opposite and
return it with your remittance for £2.25 (to cover
postage and handling) and we will print the
photograph of your choice in SEPIA (size 11 x 8
inches) and supply it in a cream mount with a
burgundy rule line (overall size 14 x 11 inches).
**Please note: photographs with a reference
number starting with a "Z" are not Frith
photographs and cannot be supplied under
this offer.**
Offer valid for delivery to one UK address only.

**PLUS: Order additional Mounted Prints
at HALF PRICE - £7.49 each** (normally £14.99)
If you would like to order more Frith prints from
this book, possibly as gifts for friends and family,
you can buy them at half price (with no
additional postage and handling costs).

PLUS: Have your Mounted Prints framed
For an extra £14.95 per print you can have your
mounted print(s) framed in an elegant polished
wood and gilt moulding, overall size 16 x
13 inches (no additional postage and handling
required).

IMPORTANT!

These special prices are only available if you use
this form to order. You must use the ORIGINAL
VOUCHER on this page (no copies permitted). We
can only despatch to one UK address. This offer
cannot be combined with any other offer.

Send completed Voucher form to:
**The Francis Frith Collection, Frith's Barn,
Teffont, Salisbury, Wiltshire SP3 5QP**

CHOOSE A PHOTOGRAPH FROM THIS BOOK

Voucher *for FREE and Reduced Price Frith Prints*

*Please do not photocopy this voucher. Only the original is valid,
so please fill it in, cut it out and return it to us with your order.*

Picture ref no	Page no	Qty	Mounted @ £7.49	Framed + £14.95	Total Cost £
		1	Free of charge*	£	£
			£7.49	£	£
			£7.49	£	£
			£7.49	£	£
			£7.49	£	£
			£7.49	£	£

Please allow 28 days for delivery. Offer available to one UK address only

* Post & handling	£2.25
Total Order Cost	£

Title of this book . . . .

I enclose a cheque/postal order for £ . . . .
made payable to 'The Francis Frith Collection'

OR please debit my Mastercard / Visa / Maestro / Amex
card, details below

Card Number

Issue No (Maestro only)   Valid from (Maestro)

Expires   Signature

Name Mr/Mrs/Ms . . . .
Address . . . .
. . . .
. . . .
. . . . Postcode . . . .
Daytime Tel No . . . .
Email . . . .

Valid to 31/12/07

Free Print – see overleaf

Would you like to find out more about Francis Frith?

We have recently recruited some entertaining speakers who are happy to visit local groups, clubs and societies to give an illustrated talk documenting Frith's travels and photographs. If you are a member of such a group and are interested in hosting a presentation, we would love to hear from you.

Our speakers bring with them a small selection of our local town and county books, together with sample prints. They are happy to take orders. A small proportion of the order value is donated to the group who have hosted the presentation. The talks are therefore an excellent way of fundraising for small groups and societies.

Can you help us with information about any of the Frith photographs in this book?

We are gradually compiling an historical record for each of the photographs in the Frith archive. It is always fascinating to find out the names of the people shown in the pictures, as well as insights into the shops, buildings and other features depicted.

If you recognize anyone in the photographs in this book, or if you have information not already included in the author's caption, do let us know. We would love to hear from you, and will try to publish it in future books or articles.

Our production team

Frith books are produced by a small dedicated team at offices in the converted Grade II listed 18th-century barn at Teffont near Salisbury, illustrated above. Most have worked with the Frith Collection for many years. All have in common one quality: they have a passion for the Frith Collection. The team is constantly expanding, but currently includes:

Paul Baron, Jason Buck, John Buck, Ruth Butler, Heather Crisp, David Davies, Isobel Hall, Julian Hight, Peter Horne, James Kinnear, Karen Kinnear, Tina Leary, Stuart Login, David Marsh, Sue Molloy, Glenda Morgan, Wayne Morgan, Kate Rotondetto, Dean Scource, Eliza Sackett, Terence Sackett, Sandra Sampson, Adrian Sanders, Sandra Sanger, Julia Skinner, Lewis Taylor, Shelley Tolcher, Lorraine Tuck and Jeremy Walker.